Write On, IRVING BERLIN!

Written by **LESLIE KIMMELMAN** ★ Illustrated by **DAVID C. GARDNER**

On a clear, cool day in September 1893, the SS Rhynland *sails into New York Harbor, past the brand-new Statue of Liberty, a gift of friendship from France several years earlier.*

The decks are crowded with people coming from many countries to live in America. Most of them are poor. Most have traveled a long, long way, across an enormous ocean, hoping that life in America will be safer, better, happier.

Look! Over there is the Baline family: Moses and Lena and their six children. Right in front—that one's Israel. He's just five years old.

Soon Israel will go by the nickname Izzy; and someday he and his marvelous music will be famous all over the world. Right now, though, he's just a tired, hungry little boy, waiting to start a new life in a new country. . . .

Israel Isidore Baline was born in 1888, in Russia.

It was a bad time and place to be Jewish. Gangs of angry men rode from village to village in pogroms, destroying Jewish homes and hurting the people who lived in them. Israel's house was burned down right in front of his eyes.

There was nothing left for the Balines in Russia. The family boarded a ship and spent eleven long days at sea. At New York's Ellis Island—the first stop for all immigrants—they went ashore. Israel's new life was about to begin.

God bless America!

Israel's first home was on New York City's crowded Lower East Side. There was little room. There was little money. There was little food.

But there was freedom.

Israel, now called Izzy, went to school. He learned English.
Still, he wasn't a very good student.

He daydreams too much,

complained his teachers.

And he sings to himself.

Back in Russia, Izzy's father had been a cantor, standing side by
side with rabbis, singing and filling synagogues with beautiful music.
So it was natural that Izzy's head, too, would be filled with music.

When Izzy was thirteen, his father died. Izzy dropped out of school and moved out of the family apartment. *There will be one less person for my mother to worry about*, he thought.

Izzy made money by—what else?—singing.

He sang in saloons.

He sang in the choruses of shows.

He sang as he waited tables in restaurants.

Then he wrote the words to his first song; someone else wrote the tune. It was called "Marie from Sunny Italy." Izzy proudly signed the music with the new name he'd chosen for himself, one that seemed just right for his new American life: *I. Berlin*. He earned 37¢.

That first song wasn't very good. So Irving, as he now called himself, kept writing. He kept getting better.

At first Irving wrote just the words. Then he started making up tunes, too. He couldn't read or write music. So he hummed the tune that was in his head, and someone else wrote it down for him.

There were <u>lots</u> of tunes in Irving's head.

Irving got a job working for a music publisher, and he kept thinking up new songs. Ragtime music was very popular in the early 1900s. It had a jazzy beat that made people want to get up and dance.

Irving decided to give ragtime a try.

"Alexander's Ragtime Band" was a smash.

Irving fell in love and married. Then tragedy struck.

His wife, Dorothy, got sick and died just a few months after their wedding. Irving was heartbroken.

But he threw himself back into his music, writing song after song. And Irving officially became an American citizen. He loved this new country of his.

God bless America!

Nothing stopped Irving from writing songs.

Not World War I.

Irving was drafted into the US Army and asked to write songs to make his fellow soldiers laugh and feel better. He wrote the words for a song called "Oh! How I Hate to Get Up in the Morning."

It was about how miserable it was for soldiers to be woken up by the bugler so early every morning. Which was pretty funny, because Irving himself had special permission to sleep late. He had told the army that he did his best work late at night and needed the mornings to rest.

Nothing stopped Irving from writing songs.

Not his new love, Ellin.

Irving wrote her a song called "Always."

He promised his love would be for always, which turned out to be true. They had a family together and were married for more than sixty years.

Irving wrote and wrote and wrote and *wrote*. He wrote music for plays, for movies, for friends, for strangers.

He scribbled ideas on napkins and on the sleeves of his shirt.

He wrote songs in elevators and in taxicabs.

He wrote songs in the bathtub.

He wrote all night long.

Nothing stopped Irving from writing.

Not World War II.

As the United States edged closer to war again, he took out and polished up a song he'd written long ago, about the land that he loved. "God Bless America" became a HUGE hit.

Some people were angry that someone Jewish, who hadn't even been born in America, had written it. Irving didn't care. He gave all the money he made from "God Bless America" to the Boy and Girl Scouts of America. It was his way of saying thank you to the country that had given him such a good life.

Soon Irving had another hit.

He told a friend, "Not only is 'White Christmas' the best song *I* ever wrote, it's the best song *anybody* ever wrote."

The year was 1942, and American soldiers were fighting fierce battles all around the world.

When they heard "White Christmas," it made them dream about home and remember all the things they were fighting for.

Again, there were some who didn't think a Jewish immigrant should write a Christmas song. But most people just let the music fill their hearts.

Irving was too old to fight in World War II. Still, he wanted to help. He performed his show "This Is the Army" for soldiers all over the world and gave every penny it made to wartime charities.

The cast was completely integrated—black and white soldiers lived, ate, and traveled together, which was rare in those days. They refused to stay or play anywhere that didn't welcome ALL of them. Irving was ahead of the times. The US Armed Forces didn't integrate until a few years after the war.

Performing in war zones was exhausting. It was dangerous. But the millions of soldiers who saw the show loved it. It made them smile in tough times.

The war ended. Irving kept writing.

He never seemed to run out of ideas.

Finally, little by little, Irving slowed down. He died when he was 101 years old, 96 long years after he'd first stepped onto the shores of his beloved United States.

His music lives on.

Author's Note

Israel Baline, sometimes spelled Beilin (1888–1989), later known as Irving Berlin, wrote more than 1,500 songs during his lifetime. He was one of a large group of Jewish American songwriters of that time that included, among others, George and Ira Gershwin, Richard Rodgers, Lorenz Hart, Jerome Kern, Alan Jay Lerner, Frederick Loewe, and Harold Arlen. Composer Jerome Kern once said, "Irving Berlin has no place in American music—he *is* American music."

Berlin had no special musical training. He couldn't read or write music or play the piano very well. He played only on black keys, which he found easier. That meant he wrote all his music in the key of F-sharp, which had only two white piano keys. Later, Berlin got a special piano that could transpose his music to other keys. Once, early in his career, he took music lessons, but after two days he decided that formal lessons might "ruin" his talent.

Berlin was well-known for staying up all night to compose. He was also famous for how much and how quickly he wrote. For his last hit show, *Annie Get Your Gun*, he wrote the song "Anything You Can Do (I Can Do Better)" in fifteen minutes—in a cab. "God Bless America," perhaps his best-known song, was originally written in 1918 during World War I, but put away for 20 years and not published until 1938, when World War II loomed on the horizon.

For service to his country, Berlin received the Medal of Merit from President Truman and the Congressional Medal of Honor from President Eisenhower. He considered the two medals his highest honors.

Berlin was a businessman as well as a musician. He helped found the American Society of Composers, Authors and Publishers (ASCAP) to protect the rights of songwriters, composers, and music publishers.

In his later years, Berlin became something of a recluse, rarely leaving home. But on Christmas Eve, in the years before he died, a small group of fans would gather outside of his New York City apartment to serenade him with "White Christmas."

Author's favorite Berlin songs

"Always"

"I Got the Sun in the Mornin' "

"I'm Putting All My Eggs in One Basket"

"Isn't This a Lovely Day?"

"What'll I Do?"

Further Reading

As Thousands Cheer: The Life of Irving Berlin
By Laurence Bergreen (Viking, 1990)

White Christmas: The Story of an American Song
By Jody Rosen (Scribner, 2002)

Irving Berlin: A Daughter's Memoir
By Mary Ellin Barrett (Simon & Schuster, 1994)

Say It with Music: The Story of Irving Berlin
By Nancy Furstinger (Morgan Reynolds Publishing Inc., 2003)

....

To listen to Irving Berlin's music, you can search the Internet by keying in "Irving Berlin's music" or visit the below links.
Disclaimer: Any website information (including links) was accessible and correct as of the publication date of this book.

www.youtube.com/watch?v=w9QLn7gM-hY [Bing Crosby singing "White Christmas"]

www.youtube.com/watch?v=b1rKQReqJZg [Kate Smith singing "God Bless America"]

www.youtube.com/watch?v=71smG5d29to [Irving Berlin performing "Oh! How I Hate to Get Up in the Morning"]

For Ray—I'll be loving you, always.

—LK

♪

For Sheree Lence, my inspiring, music-loving sister.
And for Mark — Always.

—DG

Text Copyright © 2018 Leslie Kimmelman
Illustration Copyright © 2018 David C. Gardner
Design Copyright © 2018 Sleeping Bear Press

Sleeping Bear Press

2395 South Huron Parkway, Suite 200
Ann Arbor, MI 48104
www.sleepingbearpress.com

Printed and bound in the United States.

10 9 8 7 6 5 4 3 2 1

Library of Congress Cataloging-in-Publication Data

Names: Kimmelman, Leslie, author. | Gardner, David (David Colby), 1959- illustrator.
Title: Write on, Irving Berlin! / written by Leslie Kimmelman ; illustrated by David C. Gardner.
Description: Ann Arbor, MI : Sleeping Bear Press, [2018]
Identifiers: LCCN 2017029877 | ISBN 9781585363803
Subjects: LCSH: Berlin, Irving, 1888-1989—Juvenile literature. | Composers—United States—Biography—Juvenile literature.
Classification: LCC ML3930.B446 K56 2018 | DDC 782.42164092 [B]—dc23
LC record available at https://lccn.loc.gov/2017029877